FUNDAMENTAL COUNTERPOINT

by

Hugo Norden, D.Mus.

Professor of Music Theory

SCHOOL OF FINE AND APPLIED ARTS
BOSTON UNIVERSITY

CRESCENDO PUBLISHING COMPANY

BOSTON

Standard Book Number 87597-004-4
Library of Congress Card Number 69-16932
Printed in the United States of America

TO MY DAUGHTER MARTHA

FOREWORD

This slender volume has a single and unpretentious purpose: to provide the beginner in Counterpoint with a dependable foundation upon which to build his compositional technique.

To this end the traditional five Species are called into play, largely because they make available on a systematic basis — free of any stylistic characteristics — the purely technical considerations inherent in the various time and movement relationships of concord vs. discord in an abstract idealized form.

If, by this means, the student achieves a competence in the manipulation of contrapuntal materials and develops a tehnical norm from which his individual creative style will blossom, the mission of this sketchy and all too brief introduction to the perennially fresh art of Counterpoint will have succeeded.

Hugo Norden
Boston, Massachusetts
April 2, 1969

TABLE OF CONTENTS

ABBREVIATIONS

Concerning intervals:

M	major
m	minor
P	perfect
d	diminished
A	augmented

Concerning discords:

aux.	auxiliary-note
p. n.	passing-note
s.	suspension

Concerning contrapuntal elements:

C. F.	Cantus Firmus
Cpt.	Counterpoint
Sp.	Species

INTRODUCTORY OBSERVATIONS

1. COUNTERPOINT is that branch of music theory which is concerned with the construction and the combination of melodies. It differs from Harmony in one important respect: whereas in Harmony the emphasis is on the vertical "chords," in Counterpoint the horizontal contours of the melodic lines are stressed. However, from the foregoing statement it must not be assumed that it is a case of "either - or." It is rather a difference in degree more than of kind. Both linear and vertical considerations are involved in every musical texture.

2. The term "Counterpoint" comes from the Latin "punctus contra punctum," or note against note. The emphasis here is on the word "against." Contrapuntal lines are played or sung *against,* not *with,* each other so that the prevailing spirit is one of conflict and stress. This requires skillful construction of the separate melodic lines to insure smooth effective operation.

3. Of course, this is not conflict in the violent sense. It is more nearly that of two or more lines, each with a characteristic design of its own, functioning simultaneously with a common artistic purpose. In fact, this constantly surging activity of two or more contrapuntal lines moving at once is often compared to that of quite unlike people working together. Discord and its ensuing concord are integral ingredients of the phenomena both of living and of music.

4. There are three ways in which the study of Counterpoint can be approached:

(1) through the system of the five so-called Species which present in idealized form all valid horizontal and vertical contrapuntal relationships of concord vs. discord quite apart from any particular musical or historical style;

(2) through a purely abstract study of the various contrapuntal mechanisms, such as Canon, which are derived systematically from certain mathematical formulas, and

(3) from the analysis of musical compositions in various styles without any scientific considerations.

1

This book, designed to serve as foundation for further study, is conerned mainly with the first of these three possible approaches. It is the generally acknowledged method to begin building a dependable contrapuntal technique.

5. These introductory observations define the spirit and purpose of the work at hand. But, in Counterpoint, any course — no matter how "advanced" it might purport to be — is in a sense only introductory. Counterpoint, like life itself, provides a continuing opportunity for experimentation and development.

*   *   *   *   *   *

6. Traditionally, the rhythmic unit for theoretical study of Counterpoint is the whole-note (𝅝). Against this simple background the various contrapuntal devices are set in motion. A given line of such whole-note units is called Cantus Firmus, and for practical reasons is abbreviated C. F. Against the C. F. the student constructs a new melody, the Counterpoint (abbreviated Cpt.), according to highly organized principles, or "rules." These are the materials employed in contrapuntal construction.

7. As part of these preliminary remarks, it needs to be made clear just what benefits the student can expect from this work. First, he experiences, rather than "learns," what is good and normal in musical texture. Secondly, he shares with the best composers of all ages the most respected and most widely practiced of all the theoretical disciplines. Third, he utilizes melodic and harmonic combinations with which he may otherwise remain unfamiliar, thereby becoming acquainted with numerous unexpected artistic resources. Finally, a norm is being established whereby the student can better evaluate critically his own music as well as that of others.

8. But, if at times the student feels that the rules are too restrictive, he is urged to be patient and work with them and not try to circumvent them. It is quite a common reaction, especially when beginning the study of Counterpoint, to feel that one is unduly hampered. Thus, let us approach this course with a completely open mind, and without any too firmly pre-established convictions as to what goes into the making of a successful musical composition.

CHAPTER I

CONTRAPUNTAL MELODY

1. The contours of a contrapuntal melody, in the strict academic sense, may be shaped from the following 19 intervals which — as will be seen from what is shown below— fall into 8 general classifications.

(1) *Repeated notes* (available in the 1st Species only)

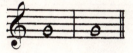

(2) *Major and Minor 2nd, up or down*

(3) *Major and Minor 3rd, up or down*

(4) *Perfect 4th, up or down*

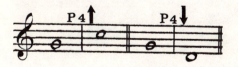

2 against 1 only and in upper voice

(5) *Diminished 5th, up or down*

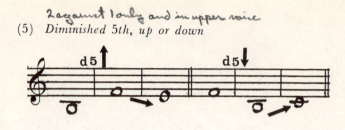

N. B. The leap of a Diminished 5th must always be followed by a move, preferably stepwise, in the opposite direction.

(6) *Perfect 5th, up or down*

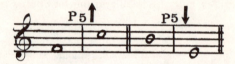

(7) *Minor 6th, up or down*

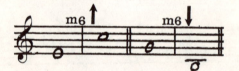

(8) *Octave, up or down*

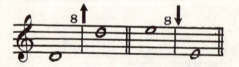

2. In contrast to the above, the following moves are *not* permitted:

(1) *Major 6th, up or down*

Disregard This particular rule

4

(2) *Major and Minor 7th, up or down*

(3) All Diminished and Augmented intervals, except the Diminished 5th (See paragraph 1 (5)).

(4) All intervals greater than an Octave.

3. Two contiguous moves in the same direction, up or down, are not permitted when they outline the following intervals:

(1) *Augmented 4th*

(2) *Major or Minor 7th*

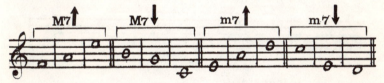

(3) *Major or Minor 9th*

4. If in such a forbidden combination of two moves one of the intervals is amongst those listed in paragraph 2, a double error will occur.

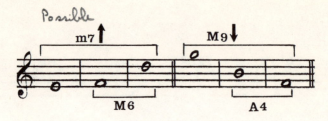

5. The following combinations of *three* contiguous moves in the same direction, up or down, are not permitted:

(1) Major and/or Minor 3rds in any combination as these would outline too conspicuously a 7th.

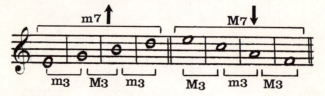

(2) Major 2nds if the extreme notes are the lowest *and* the highest points in the line as this will outline too conspicuously the Augmented 4th.

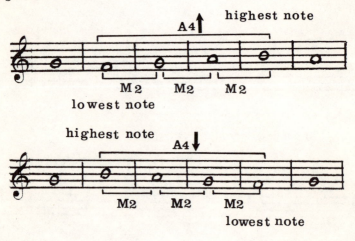

However, a series of three Major 2nds in the same direction is good if the extreme notes are *not* the lowest and highest points in the passage. The following typical passages of this type are correct:

6

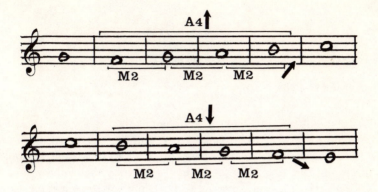

6. The normal range of a contrapuntal melody is one octave. The octave may begin and end on any note (i.e., C - C, D - D, E - E, etc).

etc.

But, it is permitted to exceed the normal range by one note at either end of the octave, thereby making available a maximum range of a 10th, thus:

CHAPTER II

THE FIRST SPECIES (NOTE AGAINST NOTE)

1. The simplest concept of counterpoint is the 1st Species, in which
the notes of the Cpt. are of equal value with those of the C. F. That
is to say, against each whole-note in the C. F. is written a whole-
note in the Cpt. according to the numerous rules that follow.
2. Concords only can serve as vertical intervals between the C. F.
and Cpt. These are as follows in two-part writing.

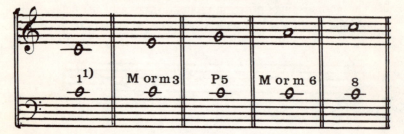

1) Permitted in the first and/or last measure only. Not So!

The 3rd, 5th, 6th, and 8ve may be expanded by an octave into the
10th, 12th, 13th, and 15th respectively; sometimes called "compound
intervals."

In general, however, it is usually better to employ such large vertical
intervals quite sparingly as the lines of the contrapuntal structure

8

are apt to wander out of control.

3. The parts may cross — that is, the lower voice going above the upper, or vice versa — when the melodic design is materially improved thereby. The point at which the voices cross must be approached and left by contrary motion. Intervals between crossed voices are referred to as 'minus' (-).

However, too much crossing of parts can confuse rather than enhance the total contrapuntal effect.

4. While crossing is permitted, overlapping is *not* acceptable. This occurs when (1) the lower voice moves in the same direction as the upper to a higher note than the preceding note in the upper voice,

and (2) the upper voice moves likewise with the lower to a lower note than the preceding note in the lower voice.

5. The two parts may not move in the same direction to a Unison, 5th, or 8ve. The following progressions are all incorrect.

They can if there is ½ step in one voice

Don't leave the unison in the same direction unless there is a half step in one direction.

1) See footnote 1) in paragraph 2, as well as paragraph 4.

6. Consecutive 5ths and 8ves are forbidden.

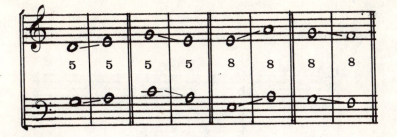

⑦ **Disregard** Likewise forbidden are the progressions 1 - 8, 8 - 1; 5 - 12, 12 - 5; 8 - 15, 15 - 8, as these are merely consecutive 5ths and 8ves in contrary motion.

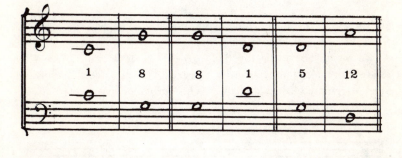

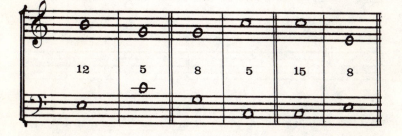

8. When the C. F. is in the lower voice, the Cpt. may begin with a unison, 5th, or 8ve above it; but, when the C. F. is in the upper voice, the Cpt. may begin only with a unison or 8ve below it. No other starting intervals are permitted.

9. One cadence formula is available: while the C. F. descends step-wise to the terminal tonic, the Cpt. ascends stepwise to the tonic from the leading-tone. Thus, the closing progression will invariably be in contrary stepwise motion to an 8ve or unison on the tonic.

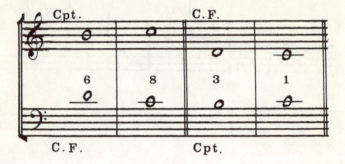

10. A special problem comes about when the C. F. moves stepwise from the fourth degree to the fifth degree of the scale, and vice versa. A 3rd or 5th above the fourth degree (IV) of the scale preceded or followed by a 3rd above the fifth degree (V) produces an objectionable Augmented 4th diagonally. This forbidden cross relation effect is known as the 'Tritone.'

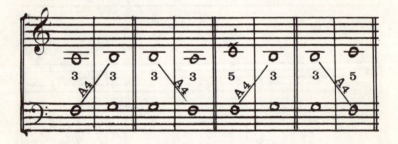

Any other combinations of intervals that contain the diagonal Tritone relationship are *not* considered as incorrect. That is, those shown above are the only wrong ones.

11. More than three 3rds or three 6ths must not be taken in succession, as such similarity of motion in the two parts tends to weaken the contrapuntal texture.

12. The rules in this chapter together with those given in Chapter I will now provide us with a working technique for the solution of problems in the 1st Species. A typical exercise might be stated thus: *write a Cpt. in the 1st Species above the following C.F.:*

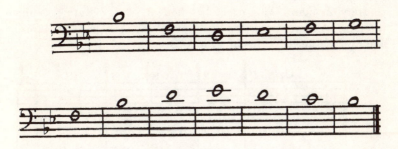

The solution could be as follows:

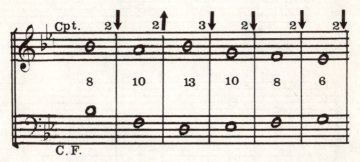

The Cpt. in the above solution stays within the quite narrow range of a 7th:

13

Note the care taken to approach the 8ve in the fifth measure by contrary motion. This could be thought of as a rather cautious working. A more venturesome solution of the same problem, utilizing more of the available resources follows.

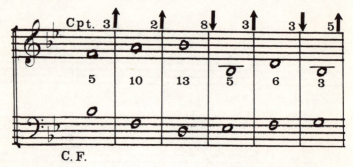

13. For writing a Cpt. in the 1st Species below the C. F. only one additional word of caution is necessary: do not use a 5th below the fourth degree of the scale (IV) as this would bring about a Diminished 5th vertically.

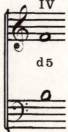

14. A typical problem would be to *write a Cpt. in the 1st Species below the following C. F.:*

The solution could be as follows:

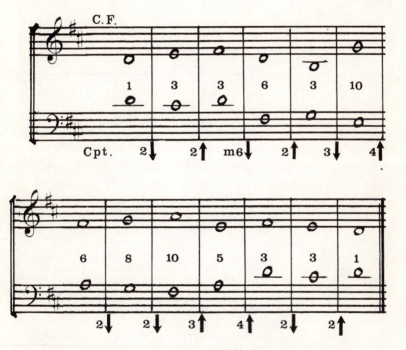

And still another working that features crossing of parts as well as a very narrow range.

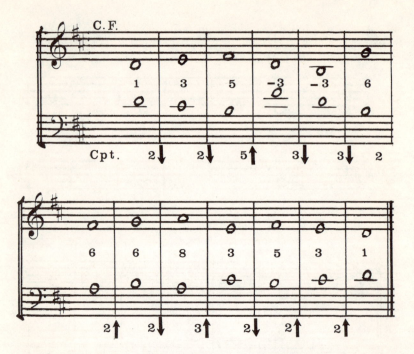

15. Do not permit your Counterpoints to ramble aimlessly. In each solution to a problem try to achieve a balanced and well-planned recognizable solution. Contrapuntal melody is highly systemized melody.

EXERCISES

Write Cpts. in the 1st Species against the following C. F.; above Nos. 1 - 5, and below Nos. 6 - 10.

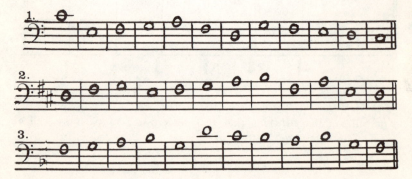

Disjunct Movement

Don't have more than 3 similar movements
Avoid Leaping in same direction in both voices at the sametime.

17

Chapter III

THE FIRST SPECIES, CONTINUED

1. Up to this point the work has been only in major keys. In minor keys many more difficulties come about. This is so because of the numerous augmented and diminished intervals contained in the harmonic form of the minor scale. In contrast thereto the major scale has only one augmented and one diminished interval, thereby making it simpler to manipulate from the contrapuntal point of view. The difference in voice-leading problems will be seen at a glance by comparing the two diagrams shown below.

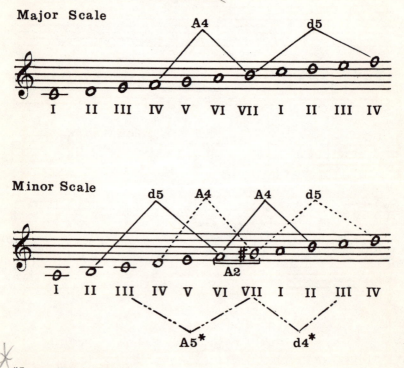

*Impossible in Major,
and forbidden in Minor.

In minor omitt the 3

18

From the above diagrams it will be seen how numerous are the possibilities that exist in minor for violating the rules given in paragraphs 2 - 5 of Chapter I.

2. Typical 1st Species Cpts. above and below the C. F. could appear as follows:

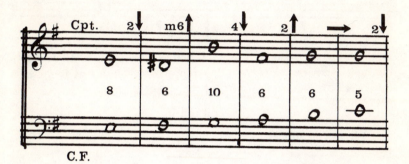

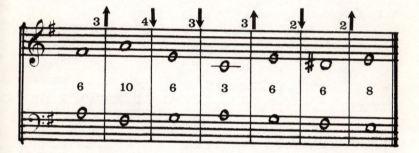

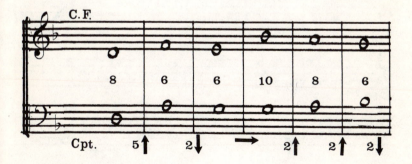

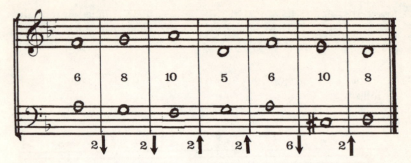

N. B. A 5th or 8ve may be approached by oblique motion — that is, one voice moving while the other repeats the note — as is the case in the sixth measure in the first of the above illustrations.

EXERCISES

Write 1st Species Cpts. against the following C. F. in Minor keys; above Nos. 1 - 3, and below Nos. 4 - 6.

CHAPTER IV

THE FIRST SPECIES, CONCLUDED

1. In the preceding three chapters Counterpoint was approached on a purely technical basis according to a given collection of "rules" regarding specific melodic and vertical situations. Now, however, a new dimension must be added: namely, awareness. It can be said that there is no such distinction as "elementary" or "advanced" Counterpoint; the student is "elementary" or "advanced" in his outlook and observations.

2. All of the Counterpoints developed so far contain numerous imitative devices that we have not paused to examine. To indicate how these imitations operate — sometimes concurrently — we shall examine the second illustration in paragraph 2 of Chapter III. But, first we must have a system of symbols for identification. Indications can be thus:

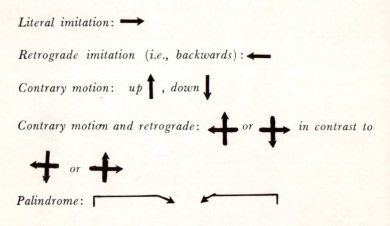

Literal imitation: ➡

Retrograde imitation (i.e., backwards): ⬅

Contrary motion: *up* ⬆ , *down* ⬇

Contrary motion and retrograde: ⬅➕ *or* ➕⬇ *in contrast to*

⬆➕ *or* ➕➡

Palindrome: ⌐➡ ⬅⌐

In the following four analytical observations of a typical exercise, the imitation is shown in large notes together with the identification code as listed above.

Observation 1: *Literal imitation*

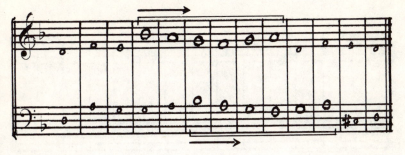

Observation 2: *Contrary motion and retrograde imitation*

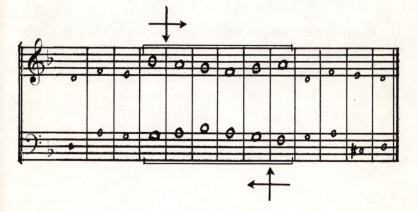

Observation 3: *Interlocking palindromes*

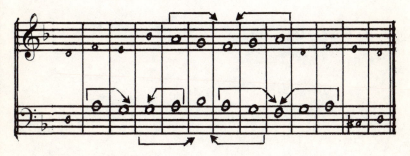

Observation 4: *Imitating three-note figures*

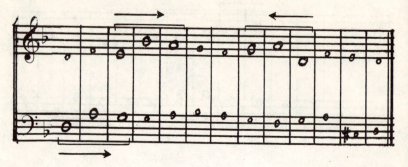

From the foregoing demonstrations it will be seen how the same basic Counterpoint can contain many different features that the composer can exploit in his finished works.

3. It is suggested that solutions to the exercises in Chapters II and III be reexamined in order to see how many interesting imitative devices they contain. In addition, new solutions may be worked out for the express purpose of bringing such imitations into play.

CHAPTER V

THE SECOND SPECIES (TWO NOTES AGAINST ONE)

1. In the 2nd Species of Counterpoint two notes are written against each note of the C. F. That is, two half-notes operate against each whole-note thus:

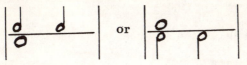

2. *Don't use* In addition to the concords as used in the 1st Species, discords[1] can now be used in four ways:

(1) on the first half-note in the measure as a *descending passing-note between two concords,*

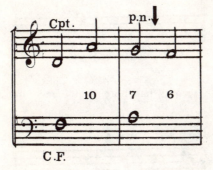

(2) on the second half-note in the measure as an *ascending passing-note,*

Use only passing Tones unaccented

[1] Discords are the Major and Minor 2nd, Perfect 4th, Major and Minor 7th and all Diminished and Augmented intervals.

25

(3) on the second half-note in the measure as a *descending passing-note*,

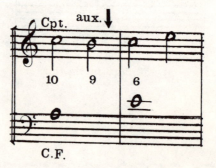

use

(4) on the second half-note in the measure as a *downward auxiliary-note*.

Don't use

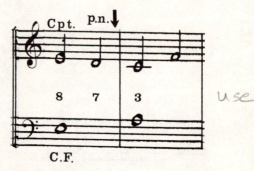

From the above illustrations two basic principles of 2nd Species dissonance can be established:

1. concords to be connected melodically by discords must be either a 3rd apart or on the same note, and

2. all accented discords (i.e., on the first half-note in the measure) must come in a descending scalewise line.

3. The unison — except in the last measure, which is always a whole-note — may occur only on the second half-note in the measure. It is good, where possible, to approach a unison by leap in the 2nd Species. To approach it stepwise would require a descending passing-note on the 2nd, which is a crude dissonance effect and is better avoided. There is, however, no hard and fast rule that prohibits such a 2 - 1 effect.

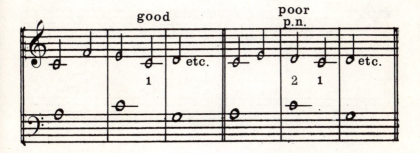

can be disregarded
4. The beginning vertical interval in this and the three Species to follow is subject to the same limitations given in the 1st Species. But, in the 2nd Species the Cpt. begins after a half measure rest.

5. The closing cadential formula is the same as that shown in Chapter II, paragraph 9. But, in the 2nd Species the next to the last note in the Cpt. must be a half-note.

6. Consecutive 5ths, 8ves and unisons (cf. paragraph 3 above) in the 2nd Species involve two contiguous measures. There are three incorrect and one correct placement possibilities as shown by the following diagram:

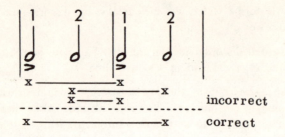

x ———————————— x incorrect
- -
x ———————————————— x correct

7. Beginning with the 2nd Species, the immediate repetition of a note is not permitted. This is purely a 1st Species effect (cf. Chapter I, paragraph 1 (1)).

8. The following is a typical 2nd Species Cpt. above a given C. F.

*) When a 6th at the first part of the measure is followed by a 5th at the second part of the measure, or vice versa, the note at the second part of the measure may be considered either as a discord (because of its melodic motion) or as a concord (because of the vertical interval). This is the only ambiguous situation possible in the 2nd Species.

28

9. The principal objective here, as in all well planned Counterpoint, is a good flowing melodic line operating with the maximum possible effect against the C. F. within the given "rules" and the horizontal and vertical restrictions which they set up.

10. One somewhat inept situation that is possible above the C. F. is impossible below the C.F.; namely, a unison at the second part of the measure approached stepwise (cf. paragraph 3 above). In order to achieve this effect below the C. F. it would be necessary to use an ascending passing-note at the first half of the measure, and this is not available.

11. A typical example of 2nd Species Cpt. below a given C. F. could appear as follows:

29

Cf. footnote to paragraph 8 above. In measure 3 above, the 5th after the 6th can be considered only as a concord since it is left by leap. A discord must be both approached and left by step.

12. Whenever discords are involved exercises in minor keys present two special problems:

(1) there is no way to descend stepwise from the raised leading-tone except to an auxiliary-note on the raised 6th degree of the scale,

(2) the raised 6th degree of the Melodic Minor Scale may be used as an ascending discord which must, of course, be on an unaccented part of the measure. This effect is shown in the third measure of the first of the two following illustrations and in the second measure of the second one.

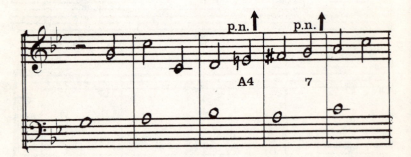

EXERCISES

Write Cpts. in the 2nd Species against the following C. F.; above Nos. 1 - 5, and below Nos. 6 - 10.

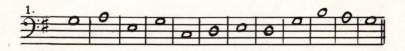

Don't more than 3 consecutive leaps in a row except when aproaching a cadence

32

CHAPTER VI

THE THIRD SPECIES (FOUR NOTES AGAINST ONE)

1. In the 3rd Species of Counterpoint four notes are written against each note of the C. F. That is, four quarter-notes operate against each whole-note thus,

2. Special consideration must be given to the first beat of each measure in two respects:

(1) it may not be a discord, and

(2) it may. not be a unison (cf. Chapter V, paragraph 3).

The latter consideration obviously does not apply to the final measure, being a whole-note. And in the initial measure the first beat is always occupied by a rest. This rest forces the Cpt. to initiate its momentum normally, on an unaccented note.

3. Discords available on the second and fourth quarters in any measure except the last are the same as on the second half-note in a 2nd Species measure, while those on the third quarter are the same as on the first half-note in a 2nd Species measure (cf. Chapter V, paragraph 2). The entire 2nd - 3rd Species dissonance system can be diagrammed as follows:

DISCORDS AVAILABLE

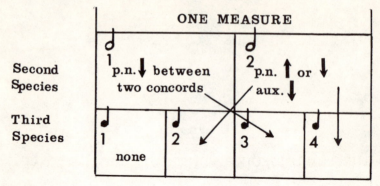

The only unaccented beat which may not be a discord is the initial note of the Cpt., i.e., the second beat in the first measure, which must be a perfect concord: unison, 5th or 8ve above the C. F., and unison or 8ve below.

4. In addition to the available discords as explained above, there are three 3rd Species figures that lie entirely outside the diagram in paragraph 3:

(1) *Nota Cambiata*, used to descend by a 2nd from the first beat of one measure to the first beat of the next.

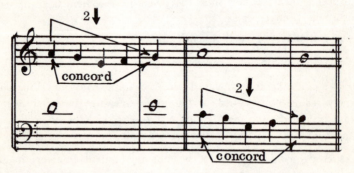

The Nota Cambiata may not begin on the leading-tone, as this would outline an Augmented 4th by two moves in the same direction.

(2) *Changing-Notes,* used to ascend by a 2nd from the first beat of one measure to the first beat of the next.

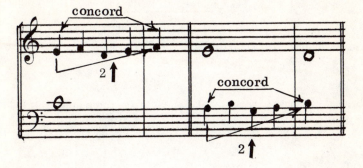

(3) *Descending Four-note Scalewise Passage,* used to descend by a 3rd or by a 5th from the first beat of one measure to the first beat of the next.

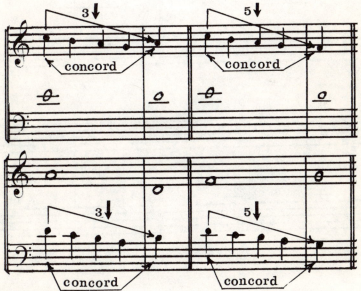

5. There are six placements, rhythmically, in which consecutive 5ths and 8ves can occur incorrectly in two contiguous measures:

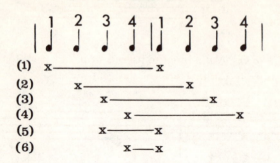

Typical instances of these six placement errors could appear as follows:

Errors (2), (3) and (4) could also occur as consecutive unisons.

6. Every measure, except the first and last, must contain at least one discord. Hence, figures such as the following are impossible.

7. In connection with paragraphs 3 and 6, a special situation is present if a 6th at the accented (that is, odd-numbered) beat is followed by a 5th at the unaccented(that is, even-numbered) beat, and vice versa, in which case the note at the unaccented beat becomes a discord (cf. footnote in paragraph 8 of Chapter V).

8. An upward leap from the first beat of any measure should be avoided.

9. After a scalewise line or arc of three or more notes, do not leap across the measure line in the same direction that the Cpt. has been moving. The following are all bad.

10. Nine cadential figures are available that can be used above the C. F. in the penultimate measure. Of the following, (4), (6), (7), and (8) are of questionable value, although quite possible within the framework of the rules for correct counterpoint.

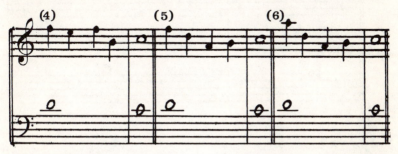

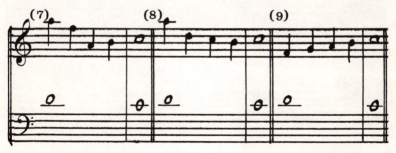

Variants of (5) and (6) could appear thus:

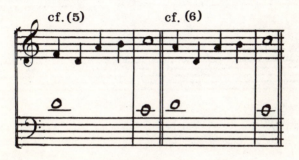

11. A typical working of a 3rd Species Cpt. problem above a C. F. could appear as follows. It is not to be expected that all of the available resources will be used in one exercise. Actually, the various figures and dissonance possibilities are merely a means to an end; namely, the writing of a smoothly flowing, graceful, and well contoured contrapuntal melody.

*) Descending Four-note Scalewise Passage   **) Nota Cambiata
***) Changing-notes

12. For writing 3rd Species Cpt. below the C. F., only one additional rule is necessary: avoid a leap of a 4th or 5th *from* an accented (odd-numbered) beat *to* an unaccented (even-numbered) beat, as this would suggest a so-called "six-four chord" within one half of a measure.

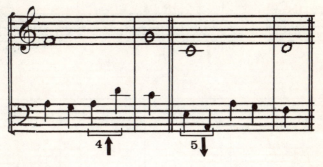

Both bad!

Thus, some figures that are acceptable above the C. F. cannot be used below the C. F.

13. But, a leap of a 4th or 5th *from* an unaccented beat *to* an accented beat is good.

All good!

14. The choice of cadences is much more limited below the C. F. Of the nine cadential formulas given in paragraph 10 above only (1) and (3) are practical below.

15. A typical working of a 3rd Species Cpt. problem below the C. F. could appear as follows:

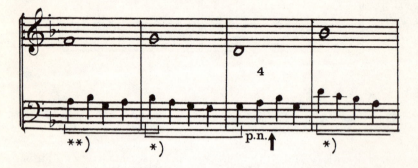

16. The 3rd Species problems — horizontal as well as vertical — in minor keys are the same as in the 2nd Species. Review paragraph 12 of Chapter V.

17. Up to this point the matter of harmony has not been mentioned. And in the purest sense Counterpoint should not be thought of as an embellished form of harmony, actual or implied. On the other hand, the rules which have already been given, as well as those that are to follow, will be more meaningful if interpreted in the light of the

harmony that is more or less inevitably implied by the simultaneous operation of a C. F. and Cpt. within the intervallic framework set forth in this course.

18. Five harmonic effects are available in Strict Counterpoint:
    (1) Major triad in root position
    (2) Minor triad in root position
    (3) Major triad in its 1st inversion
    (4) Minor triad in its 1st inversion
    (5) Diminished triad in its first inversion, provided the root of the triad is placed above the fifth.

19. One or two harmonies may be present within one measure; but if there are two, the second of the two harmonies may enter only at the third quarter. A new harmony may *not* be introduced at an unaccented (even-numbered) beat. Thus, regardless of the speed of the contrapuntal melody, the implied harmonies can progress in only three rhythmic dimensions:

$$(1) \mid o \mid \qquad (2) \mid d \; d \mid \qquad (3) \mid d \; d \mid d \; d \mid$$

The following illustration demonstrates these three rhythmic possibilities as they may occur within one exercise:

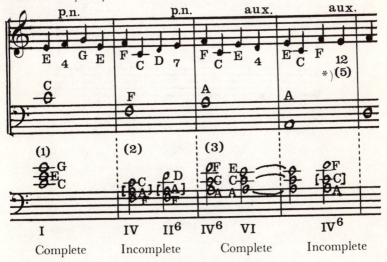

Bracketed notes in the above harmonic analysis are present by implication only; they do not actually appear in the Cpt.

*) The fact that this 5th must be considered as a discord against the implied harmony is in line with and is confirmed by what is shown in paragraph 7 above.

20. From what is shown above it will be seen that in writing a Cpt. against a given C. F. one has the opportunity to outline
    (1)   complete or incomplete harmonies, and
    (2)   definite or ambiguous harmonies.
In the case of a 5th or 6th the harmony is definitely fixed since the only other note that could be added is a 3rd above the bass within the harmonic possibilities listed in paragraph 18 above.

A 3rd (or 10th) or an 8ve is harmonically ambiguous and can be seen either as an incomplete triad in root position or as an incomplete triad in the 1st inversion.

21. The three figures shown in paragraph 4 above imply in all cases only one harmony per measure; namely, that suggested by the first interval in the measure.

22. When the Cpt. is below the C. F. the implied harmony may not always be seen quite so clearly. This is especially true when the Cpt. features a descending passing-note on the third beat, in which case the note at the fourth beat determines the implied harmony for the entire second half of the measure. The following illustration shows how this situation comes about.

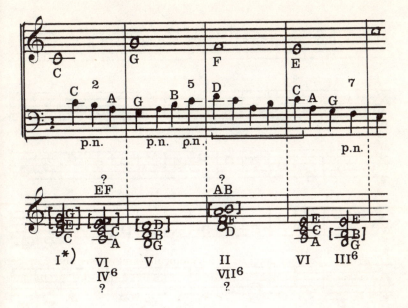

Incomplete   Incomplete   Incomplete (?) Complete Incomplete

*) First and last harmonies are always considered as I in root position.

EXERCISES

Write Cpts. in the 3rd Species against the following C. F.; above Nos. 1 - 4 and below Nos. 5 - 8.

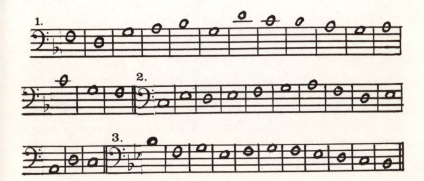

Should additional exercises be required, any of the C. F. provided for any other Species may be used.

Chapter VII

THE THIRD SPECIES, CONCLUDED

1. This chapter concerns three specific refinements in 3rd Species Counterpoint that lie rather beyond the "rules" given in the last five chapters. While one can write "correct" counterpoint on what has gone before, the suggestions that follow will improve the contrapuntal line artistically. That is to say, the following observations are intended to add style, elegance, and sophistication to what otherwise may be merely commonplace and pedantic 3rd Species Counterpoint.

2. The first of the three considerations involves leaping across the measure line. Such a leap can be taken under three specific conditions:
   (1) after a leap in the opposite direction
   (2) after a leap in the same direction,
   (3) after a scalewise line in the opposite direction.
Artistically speaking, (1) can be considered as the most successful, (2) as second best, and (3) as somewhat less good. This classification is made purely on an artistic, and not functional, basis. Correctness, as such, does not enter into it.

3. In the preceding chapter there are three illustrations of condition (1):
   paragraph 11 — musical example measures 5-6 and 7-8
   paragraph 15 — musical example measures 6-7
No further illustrations of this particular condition need be given at this time.

4. Conditions (2) and (3)are not illustrated previously since they represent something less than the very best in 3rd Species thinking. However, when employed, the following restrictions should be observed.

5. When an ascending leap across the measure line follows an ascending leap, the first of these two contiguous leaps should be approached from the opposite direction, preferably scalewise. And the same restriction holds true when a descending leap across the measure line follows a descending leap.

The following, although there is no violation of a rule, are less successful from the point of view of melodic design.

6. If an ascending leap across the measure line is preceded by a descending scalewise line, the third beat of the measure from which the leap is made must be a descending passing-note.

A comparable situation is impossible in the opposite direction.

7. The second of the three 3rd Species refinements mentioned in paragraph 1 concerns the highest or lowest note of a scalewise arc. It is not good to let the highest note of an arc be the leading-tone, nor the lowest the subdominant.

Both bad!

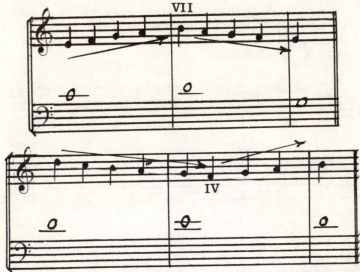

Better solutions would be:

8. The third of the three refinements concerns the mixture of scale-wise motion and leaps in the same direction. In general, such a

broken line makes for poor contrapuntal melody. This is the reason why the last two illustrations in paragraph 5 are branded as "less successful." It is better, if possible, to place the leap at the beginning of the passage, and then proceed scalewise thereafter. The following show how this principle can be carried out.

9. The foregoing observations can be considered as a sort of postscript to Chapter VI. For exercises to put these refinements into practice, any of the C. F. given so far may be used.

CHAPTER VIII

THE FOURTH SPECIES

(TWO NOTES, SYNCOPATED AGAINST ONE)

1. The 4th Species of Counterpoint consists of two notes against one, but tied across the measure line to create syncopation.

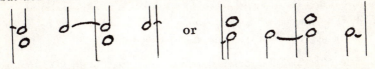

The resources of the 4th Species are limited to three devices.

2. The first and most important of the three 4th Species devices is the Suspension. When the concord at the second part of a measure is one note lower that the concord at the second part of the measure immediately preceding it, the earlier of these two concords can be tied across the measure line to form an accented discord, which is the suspension that resolves downward by step to the second concord. The following illustration shows how this comes about.

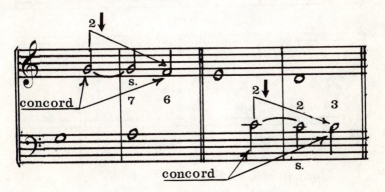

Because of the intervals involved in the suspension and its resolu-

51

tion, the above illustrations would be spoken of as a "7-6 suspension" and a "2-3 suspension" respectively.

3. The total list of available suspensions is as follows:

Above the C. F.: 7-6, 4-3, 9-8*), 6-5*) **)

Below the C.F.: 2-3, 4-5*) ***), 5-6*) **)

*) Two of any of these may not be taken in succession becaues of the resulting consecutive 5ths or 8ves.

**) May be considered either as a suspension or as a tie. See paragraph 5 below.

***) Not good below the fourth degree (IV) of the major scale, nor below the fourth (IV) or sixth (VI) degrees of the minor scale, as in all three cases the suspension would resolve to a Diminished 5th.

N. B. The intervals of a 2nd *above* the C. F. and a 7th *below* the C. F. are never used as suspensions in strict counterpoint.

4. The intervals of suspension may be increased by an 8ve; that is, 4-3 expanded to 11-10, 2-3 to 9-10, etc.

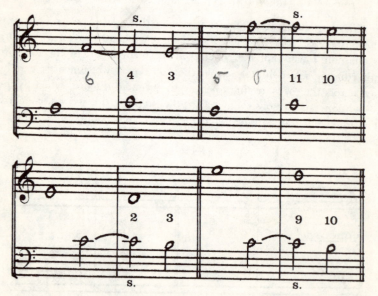

5. The second 4th Species device is a Tie, which consists simply of a concord at the second part of one measure tied to another concord at the first part of the next measure. A tie can be left either by leap

or stepwise (cf. footnote **) in paragraph 3 above).

Break suspensions stepwise & Downwards

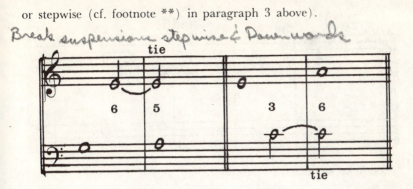

6. The third 4th Species device consists of an occasional pair of notes in the 2nd Species; that is, not tied across the measure line. Three untied notes may precede the whole-note in the last measure.

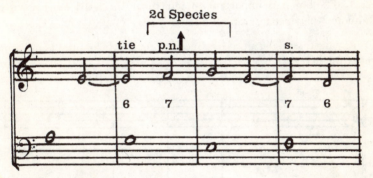

7. A typical working of a 4th Species problem above a C. F. could appear as follows.

53

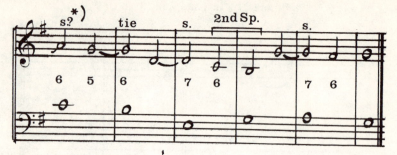

*) See footnote **) in paragraph 3.

In general, the counterpoint will be more powerful if there are more suspensions than ties.

8. No other instructions are needed for writing the 4th Species below the C. F. But it is important to remember the restrictions given in footnote ***) in paragraph 3 above.

9. A typical working of a 4th Species problem below the C. F. could be as follows.

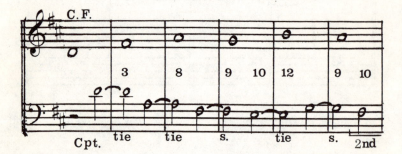

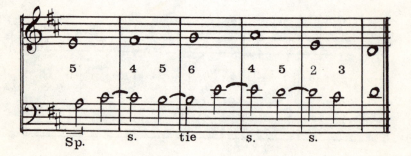

EXERCISES

Write Cpts. in the 4th Species against the following C. F.; above Nos. 1 - 5, and below Nos. 6 - 10.

Chapter IX

THE FIFTH SPECIES (FLORID)

1. The 5th Species of Counterpoint combines all that has been taken up thus far plus certain effects in eighth-notes. This is what is usually referred to as "florid" counterpoint. However, the 1st Species is not employed except in the final measure because it would be unthinkable to have an entire measure with no activity. The chief characteristic of the 5th Species is to have as much motion and vitality as possible within the available resources — vertical, melodic, and rhythmic.

2. Groups of two eighth-notes may appear on the second and/or fourth quarters of a measure in the following five rhythmic patterns:

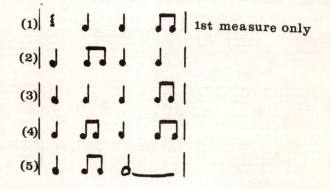

Eighth-notes must be approached and left stepwise, and must proceed likewise. In other words, do not leap *into, out of,* or *between* eighth-notes. Eighth-notes *never* occur at the first or third quarters.

3. It is normal, and usually best, if a half-note at the second part of a measure is tied over into the next measure. But, if there are two half-notes in a measure (that is, there being no quarter- or eighth-note motion) such a tie is not obligatory. In the following three figures the half-note *must* be tied.

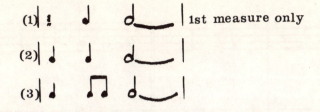

(1) 🎵 ♩ ♩⌣⌣ | 1st measure only

(2) ♩ ♩ ♩⌣ |

(3) ♩ ♫ ♩⌣ |

4. The following four figures are *not* used:

(1) ▬ ♩ ♩ | 1st measure only

(2) ▬ ♩ ♫ | 1st measure only

(3) 𝅝 ♩ ♩ |

(4) 𝅝 ♩ ♫ |

This restriction is made because in contrapuntal melody new motion in quick notes after a longer note or rest does not normally begin on an accented beat.

5. Suspensions may be embellished melodically and rhythmically by means of four ornamental resolutions:

Basic
Suspension

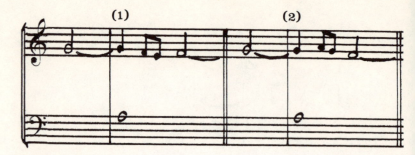

*) Not good in 4-3 or 6-5 above the C.F. or in 5-6 below the C. F.

6. The same ornamental resolution should not appear in two or more contiguous measures. When several suspensions come in succession, the ornaments should be mixed and contrasted as much as possible. For instance, not this

but this.

The five suspension forms — the basic suspension and four ornamental resolutions — can be mixed in 120 different orders when all five are used in succession.

7. If, for any reason, it is either not desired or impractical to tie the half-note of the resolution, the resolution may be a quarter-note on the third beat of the measure and the fourth beat occupied by a quarter-note or by two eighth-notes. The following illustrations show how rhythms (2), (3), and (4) as given in paragraph 2 can be utilized in this connection.

8. The melodic design of ornamental resolution (2) as shown in paragraph 5 above can serve a purpose not shared by the other three ornamental resolution figures. It can be a tie (that is, a concord) with the third beat becoming an accented descending passing-note in accordance with the 3rd Species discord principles (cf. Chapter VI, paragraph 3). This can come about as follows:

9. While suspensions with their ornamental resolutions and ties provide the basic materials for 5th Species motion, it is entirely possible to employ eighth-notes in other ways so long as they meet the conditions stated in paragraph 2. The following uses are typical.

While no hard and fast rule exists as to a good proportion between tied and untied measures, it is common academic practice *not* to write *more than two* rhythmically identical untied figures in succession. In the 5th Species the emphasis is on achieving the maximum in variety and energy, the latter chiefly by means of dissonance.

10. The following may be considered as a typical solution to a 5th Species problem above the C. F. While it goes without saying that not all of the 5th Species resources can be utilized in one short exer-

cise, the student is urged to study this example carefully and take "count of stock," so to speak, as to how many of the available devices are present and how many are left unused.

Measures 1, 7, and 11 illustrate the principle that measures containing a half-note and/or rest (first measure only) do not also have to contain a discord unless one is desired. However, measures without discords are apt to sound weak and should occur only relatively seldom unless, for artistic reasons, very few discords are wanted.

11. Herewith are completed the basic rules for strict counterpoint in two parts against a given C. F.

12. No instructions beyond those in paragraphs 1 - 10 above are needed for writing 5th Species Cpt. below the C. F. However, the restrictions concerning suspensions as set forth in Chapter VIII, paragraph 3, should be kept in mind.

13. The following is a typical solution of a 5th Species problem below the C. F.

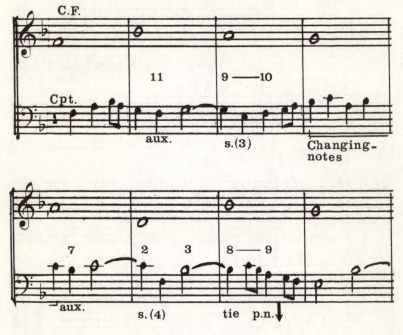

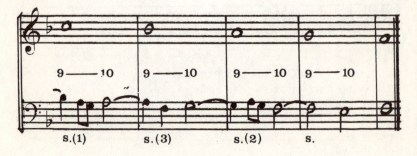

14. In minor keys 5th Species Cpt. above the C. F. presents one suspension problem that does not exist in major. This can be stated as follows:

the raised leading-tone cannot be used as a suspension since there is no way for it to resolve stepwise downward (cf. Chapter V, paragraph 12 (1).)

15. As in the 3rd Species, the raised sixth degree of the ascending melodic minor scale will be used only as an ascending discord.

16. Except for the above observations no new instructions are needed. The following is a typical 5th Species working in minor.

17. 5th Species Cpt. below the C. F. in a minor key is further restricted by the fact that the 4-5 suspension is impractical against the fourth (IV) and sixth (VI) degrees of the scale. See Chapter VIII, paragraph 3, footnote ***). Except for this observation, no new instructions are needed.

18. The following will serve as a typical working of a 5th Species problem below a C. F. in minor.

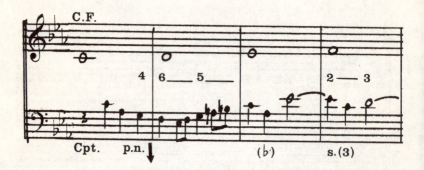

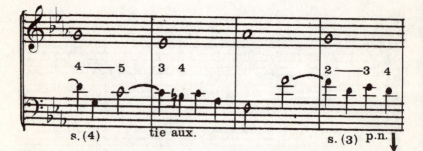

In reference to what is shown in Chapter VI, paragraphs 19 - 22, measures 2 and 3 above must be thought of as each implying two different harmonies per measure. This is most subtle in measure 3 wherein the half-note E-flat cannot be considered as belonging to the A-flat triad (although it may sound so!) as this would suggest a six-four chord, which is unavailable except as a discord formation in strict counterpoint.

EXERCISES

Write Cpts. in the 5th Species against the following C. F.; above Nos. 1-5, and below Nos. 6-10.

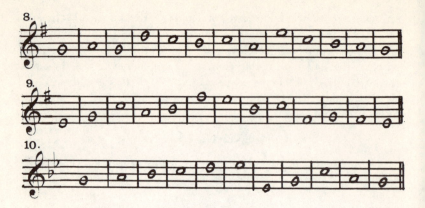

Chapter X

TWO PARTS IN THE FIFTH SPECIES
WITHOUT A GIVEN C. F.

1. Herewith is undertaken an entirely new kind of problem: namely, original composition without a given C. F. to serve as a predetermined support for the Cpt. The music to be written will be for two voices or instruments or for a keyboard instrument and will exploit to the limit of the student's skill and imagination the resources of 5th Species Counterpoint.

2. Five rhythms not previously available are now necessary in order to achieve a continuous flow of contrapuntal texture:

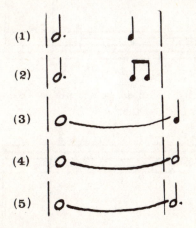

None of the above rhythms may be used unless the counterpointing part (i.e., the accompanying part) strikes a note at the third beat of the measure; and rhythms (3), (4), and (5) are not to be used unless the other part strikes a note at the beginning of the measure to which the whole-note is tied. In other words, in two-part writing of this kind both parts should not be stationary at an accent since this would result in an interruption of the contrapuntal activity.

3. A note may not be tied to a note of greater value than itself; that is, a half-note cannot be tied to a dotted half-note or to a whole-note. Therefore the following two rhythms are impossible.

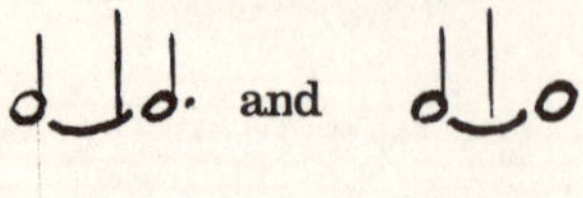

4. Two discords operating at once may not produce another discord. This rule, however, concerns chiefly unaccented passing-notes and auxiliary-notes. To illustrate, the following passage is good because the two passing-notes on the fourth beat of the measure strike together as a 3rd.

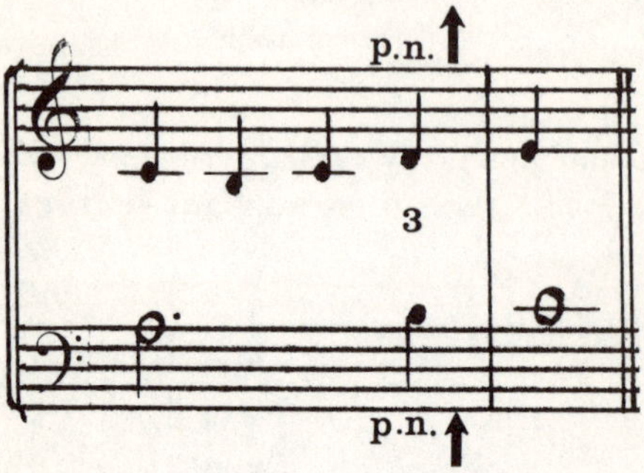

However, the following would *not* be acceptable since the two discords on the fourth beat strike together as a 7th.

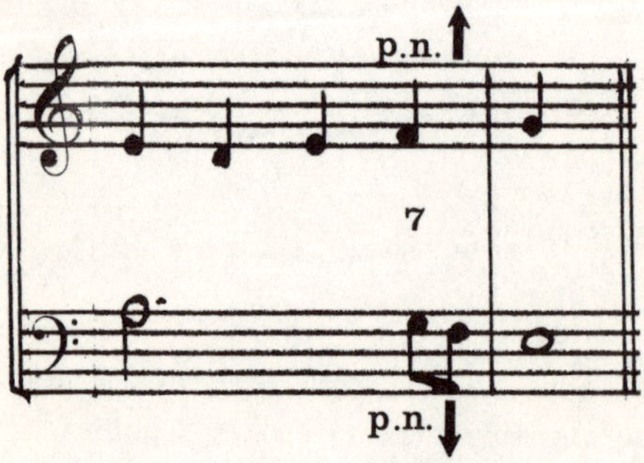

5. In writing two parts in 5th Species Counterpoint without a given C. F., each new measure requires two basic decisions out of a list of four available decisions. These can be formalized as follows:

1st Decision: *Which part is to serve as C. F. for that measure?* It can be either the upper or lower, but for purposes of illustration the lower voice is being chosen to serve as C. F. for the first measure.

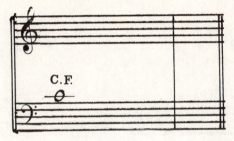

2nd Decision: *Shall the C. F. note be tied or not tied into the next measure?* If the answer is "yes," the note to which it ties can be written in as follows. The exact time value will depend upon future decisions.

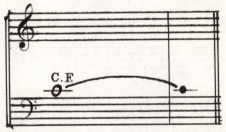

3rd Decision: *Is the note to which the C. F. note ties to be a concord or discord?* If the latter, it will automatically become a suspension and must be resolved accordingly. A suitable note to serve as C. F. for the suspension will then be written in in the other voice.

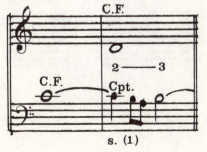

s. (1)

Now the counterpointing part must be filled in in the first measure so that the second measure is approached correctly. The following illustration shows a number of possibilities for completing the first measure in the present problem.

If, however, it is desired to tie the C. F. note of the first measure to a concord, then the second will begin with a tie, which does not require resolution.

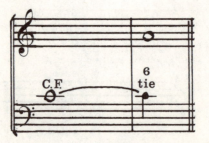

An assortment of suitable workings of the first measure leading to the concord at the beginning of the second measure follows.

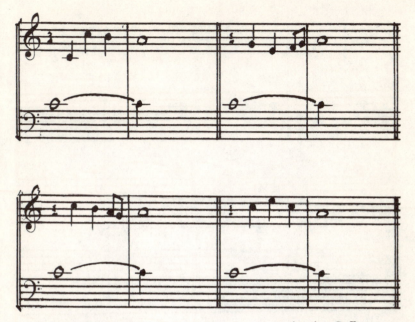

4th Decision: If it is preferred not to tie the C. F. note into the next measure, then it must be decided **WHERE** *to go and* **HOW** *to get there by means of rhythms (1) or (2) as shown in paragraph 2 above.* Suppose the decision has been made to bring the C. F. note down a 2nd into the next measure; it could be done as follows:

Now the counterpointing voice must be filled in. Again, an asortment of possible workings of the first measure follows.

6. Scalewise directional figures for bringing the C. F. note into the next measure without tie can be catalogued as follows:

(1) *Up a 2nd*

(2) *Down a 2nd*

(3) *Up a 3rd*   (4) *Down a 3rd*

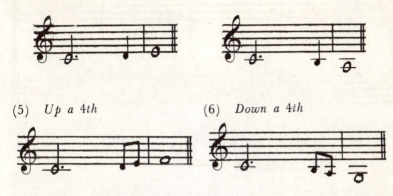

(5) *Up a 4th*   (6) *Down a 4th*

7. Should a quarter-note on the fourth beat of the measure be approached and left by leap, care must be taken that (1) it does not imply a new chord, and (2) it does not suggest a six-four chord (cf. Chapter VI, paragraph 12).

8. Each subsequent measure must be calculated by the same process. The following is a short example of this kind by contrapuntal writing. Reconstruct the decisions and dissonant effects demonstrated by each measure.

Examine the above Cpt. carefully from the following points of view:

    (1) how each measure is introduced,

    (2) what takes place within each measure, and

    (3) how each measure is left.

Account for every note in relation to the rule which it represents. In composition of this type nothing is left to chance; everything is calculated.

EXERCISES

Beginning as follows compose a short piece (between 16 - 20 measures) in two-part 5th Species Cpt. for two voices or instruments. Bring the composition to a satisfactory close with a correct and effective cadence. Think of this as music, *not* as an exercise!

It is expected that the student will invent original beginnings and then develop them into finished compositions of whatever length he may desire.

CHAPTER XI

THE FIFTH SPECIES WITHOUT A GIVEN C.F., CONCLUDED

1. To the type of contrapuntal writing demonstrated in Chapter X can be added another dimension: *imitation*. While no new technical instructions are required, considerably more is demanded of the composer in two respects:

    (1) familiarity with all available resources, and

    (2) inventive ingenuity sufficient to utilize the available resources for artistic purposes.

2. The following example of imitative counterpoint features three themes: the principal one (indicated by the solid line) occurring five times — twice in the lower voice and three times in the upper, and two shorter themes, each occurring twice (indicated by dotted lines and dot-and-dash lines respectively).

3. No explanatory notations are provided on the music that follows, but the student is expected to study every measure in the light of the three points of view given at the end of paragraph 8 in Chapter X.

The numerous imitations as they overlap and interlock help to produce a tightly knit and highly unified texture.

4. A project such as the one shown in paragraph 3 above becomes more difficult and restricted in a minor key. Nevertheless, no new instructions are required, only more resourcefulness, imagination and ingenuity. An example for analysis follows.

The vertical arrows indicate the imitation in contrary motion. Attention is called especially to measures 6 - 8 and 11 - 13. In these two passages the lower voice has exactly the same material while the upper voice is not the same both times. Naturally, the harmonic implications and the general contrapuntal effect is quite different in these two passages with the identical lower part.

5. One further dimension can be added to this kind of two-part contrapuntal composition without a given C. F.; namely *modulation*. However, this is not modulation in the harmonic sense where chords

are involved. Rather, this is modulation by melodic implication and is achieved by the use of strategically placed accidentals, chiefly on unaccented discords.

6. For present requirements four specific accidentals will be employed:

>   (1) lowered leading-tone (VII) = subdominant (IV) of the subdominant key, or submediant (VI) of the relative minor of the subdominant key,
>
>   (2) raised subdominant (IV) = leading-tone (VII) of the dominant key,
>
>   (3) raised dominant (V) = leading-tone (VII) of the relative minor key, and
>
>   (4) raised tonic (I) = leading-tone (VII) of the relative minor of the subdominant key.

While other accidentals can be used, the present assignment will be limited to the above to avoid the possibility of going too far afield from the original key. The following melodic fragments will show how these accidentals can be applied to the key of C major.

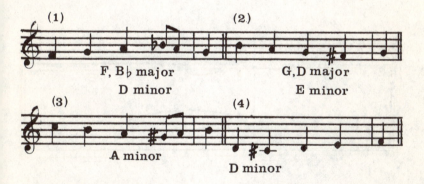

N. B. These Roman numerals refer to scale degrees, not chords.

7. Chromatic alterations to modulate away from a given minor key concern mainly the lowering of the raised leading-tone, which places the tonality automatically in that of the relative major key. For instance, if in the key of A minor the G-sharp is lowered to G-natural the result is merely that of C major. However, by C major in this context is not meant the audible effect as much as it is a basis for chromatic calculation.

8. Two suggestions are in order for the artistic use of such modulatory accidentals:

> (1) lowered notes normally descend stepwise, while raised notes ascend; and
>
> (2) a chromatized note must not set up a cross relation with a natural note (i.e., naturally within the key) which occurs too soon before or after it. Such spacing of natural and chromatized notes is, of course, largely a matter of artistic purpose and personal taste; but, as a "rule of thumb" it might be said that they should not generally be as close as in two adjacent measures, and never in the same measure. But, if it is desired to feature an abrupt or heavily chromatic texture, the above suggestion can be ignored. However, a natural and a chromaticized note must not sound at once.

9. The following example shows how such modulatory effects can be used in writing music for two parts in the 5th Species without a given C. F.

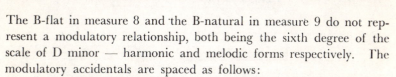

The B-flat in measure 8 and the B-natural in measure 9 do not represent a modulatory relationship, both being the sixth degree of the scale of D minor — harmonic and melodic forms respectively. The modulatory accidentals are spaced as follows:

> (1) F-sharp, measure 2, upper voice, followed by F-natural in measure 4, upper voice (no F precedes the F-sharp),
>
> (2) B-flat, measure 5, lower voice, preceded by B-natural in measure 3, lower voice (no B between B-flats in measures 5 and 8),
>
> (3) C-sharps in measures 7 and 9 preceded by C-natural in measure 5, lower voice and followed by C-natural in measure 12, upper voice,
>
> (4) G-sharp, measure 11, lower voice, preceded by G-natural in measure 8, lower voice (no G after G-sharp).

Even with this careful spacing it may be felt that in performance the modulations implied by the accidentals in the above passages follow one another too closely.

10. It is left to the student to identify the C. F. decisions, imitations, suspensions, etc. in the above example.

EXERCISES

Using as beginnings the following, write pieces of at least 20 measures demonstrating the four modulation effects listed in paragraph 6 above in addition to whatever interesting imitation effects can be brought in. Since this concludes the work in two-part counterpoint the projects below should be regarded as a review of all that has gone before and should represent the most serious and thoughtful work. This is in no sense of the word an "exercise;" it is a sincere artistic effort written within certain specific idiomatic and technical limitations.

Invent original beginnings and develop them into finished compositions with as much skill and imagination as possible.

Chapter XII

COUNTERPOINT IN THREE PARTS

1. This chapter deals with the problem of writing two Cpts. in the 1st Species against a given C. F. Herewith is produced a polyphonic texture of three contrapuntal parts — C. F. + 2 Cpts. — all in notes of equal duration.

2. The remaining chapters are given over to the technique of writing counterpoint in more than two parts. This can be thought of in two ways: as "counterpoint in more than two parts" or as "counterpoint in three or more parts." While this may seem like semantic hair-splitting, it does actually represent two quite different points of view. These should be clear as the work progresses.

3. All multi-voiced contrapuntal writing consists of a specific number of concurrent and interlocking two-part Cpts. according to the following table:

    3-part Cpt. = 3 2-part Cpts.
    4-part Cpt. = 6 2-part Cpts.
    5-part Cpt. = 10 2-part Cpts.
    6-part Cpt. = 15 2-part Cpts.
    7-part Cpt. = 21 2-part Cpts.
    8-part Cpt. = 28 2-part Cpts.
    etc.

How this principle operates can be readily seen from the familiar four-part writing for mixed voices as is found in any hymnal. The 6 2-part Cpts. as found in such four-part scoring can be listed thus:

    (1) Bass-Tenor
    (2) Bass-Alto
    (3) Bass-Soprano
    (4) Tenor-Alto
    (5) Tenor-Soprano
    (6) Alto-Soprano

From what is shown above it becomes immediately apparent that complexity increases very considerably with the addition of each new part to the contrapuntal fabric.

4. From the above tabulations emerges the so-called *"two-voice principle"* on which this and the remaining work is based:

> *In any multi-voiced structure, if all of the component two-part Cpts. are correct, it follows that the structure as a whole is correct.*

Conversely, any error will appear in one of the two-part Cpts.

5. The harmonic material available in strict counterpoint in more than two parts still consists of the five formations listed in paragraph 18 of Chapter VI.

6. The list of concords given in paragraph 2 of Chapter II is now expanded as follows: *the Perfect 4th and the Augmented 4th become concords when they occur in two upper voices.* But, they still remain as discords between the lowest and some upper voice. Thus, the six-four chord is impossible in the 1st Species, and in the remaining Species it can come about only as a dissonant effect.

7. Paragraph 5 of Chapter II requires one modification in order to make it applicable to three-part counterpoint: *two parts may move in the same direction to an 8ve if one of the voices ascends by Perfect 4th and the other by Minor 2nd.* The following illustration is typical.

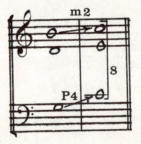

This makes available the Authentic Cadence. In more than three parts it is often necessary to relax the restrictions against hidden 5ths and 8ves somewhat. But, for the present, only the specific liberty mentioned above will be permitted.

8. The unison may be used only in the first and/or last measures. The 8ve, however, may be freely used provided it is approached correctly.

9. The following illustrations show a C. F. and two 1st Species Cpts. in three arrangements: first, with the C. F. in the Bass; secondly, with the C. F. in the Alto, and finally, with the C. F. in the Soprano. The more important imitations are indicated in the usual way (cf. Chapter IV).

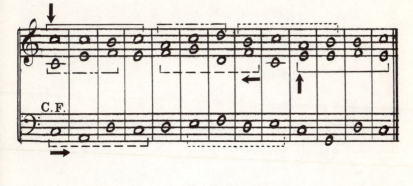

* - - - * Crossing of parts.

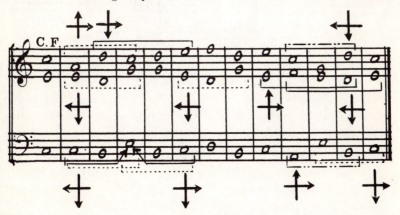

The first and last measures normally contain the I triad in root position, complete or incomplete. The next to the last measure may contain the V triad in root position, V₆ or VII₆.

10. Except for the additional resources made available in paragraphs 6 and 7 no new instructions are required for the work that follows.

EXERCISES

Write two 1st Species Cpts. against each of the following C.F. as indicated. Indicate carefully all imitations as shown in paragraph 9 above.

1. C. F. in Bass, Cpts. in Alto and Soprano

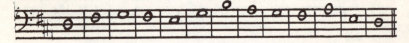

2. C. F. in Alto, Cpts. in Bass and Soprano

3. C. F. in Soprano, Cpts. in Bass and Alto

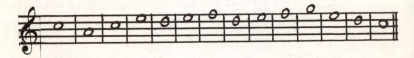

For additional exercises any C. F. from previous chapters may be used.

CHAPTER XIII

COUNTERPOINT IN THREE PARTS, CONTINUED

1. The operation of the *"two-voice principle"* is seen more clearly when two different Species are written against a C. F. The following illustration is structured thus:

> Bass: 3rd Species
> Alto: C. F.
> Soprano: 1st Species

Hence, the Bass and Alto must make correct 3rd Species Cpt.; the Bass and Soprano must likewise make correct 3rd Species Cpt., while the Alto and Soprano must be in correct 1st Species Cpt. The 1st Species Cpt. in the Soprano actually becomes another C. F. against which the Bass moves in 3rd Species Cpt.

* - - - * Crossing of parts in two upper voices.

2. The C. F. and the two different Cpts. can be written in six vertical arrangements. Using C. F., 1st Species, and 3rd Species these possibilities can be listed thus:

(1) 3rd Species	(3) 3rd Species	(5) 1st Species
1st Species	C. F.	C. F.
C. F.	1st Species	3rd Species

(2) 1st Species	(4) C. F.	(6) C. F.
3rd Species	3rd Species	1st Species
C. F.	1st Species	3rd Species

The example in paragraph 1 demonstrates vertical arrangement (5). In any one of the six arrangements, the contrapuntal problems are much the same.

3. When the 5th Species is written against a C. F. and a 1st Species Cpt., one new restriction must be added: *do not place a 9 - 8 suspension between two upper voices*. That is to say, the 9 - 8 suspension is good only between the lowest and some upper voice.

4. When the 5th Species is involved, application of the "two-voice principle" can bring about vertical situations which are perfectly correct contrapuntally, but which do not fall within the five harmonic effects listed in paragraph 18 of Chapter VI (cf. Chapter XII, paragraph 5). This comes about when a tied note followed by ornamental resolution figure (2) results in a suspension against one voice and a tie against the other voice. The following example, broken up into its component two-part Cpts., shows how this curious harmonic situation can happen. From the chordal point of view the following illustration has a 7th chord in its first inversion on the first beat of the measure and a six-four chord on the third beat.

5. The following illustration is a typical combination of a C.F., 1st Species, and 5th Species. The vertical arrangement of the three

parts can be identified from the list of six possibilities given in paragraph 2 above. Note how unity is achieved through the recurring melodic figure in the 5th Species, and through the palindromic beginning and ending of the 1st Species part. It is left to the student to identify each contrapuntal device used.

EXERCISES

Write combinations of 1st and 3rd Species and 1st and 5th Species against the following C. F. in all six vertical arrangements listed in paragraph 2 above. When the C. F. is placed in the Alto, transpose it up one 8ve thus,

and when it is placed in the Soprano, transpose it up another 8ve to begin as follows.

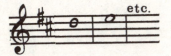

5.

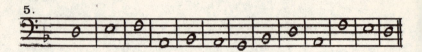

The 3rd and 5th Species must be checked out so that it becomes certain that they operate correctly both against the C. F. and against the Cpt. in the 1st Species. This brings into play two 3rd Species or two 5th Species mechanisms operating concurrently.

The 2nd Species and 4th Species can be written against a C. F. and 1st Species in the same way as has been shown above with the 3rd Species and 5th Species but, in general, the results are not as interesting.

Chapter XIV

COUNTERPOINT IN THREE PARTS, CONTINUED

1. When two Cpts. are written against a C. F. and neither one of the Cpts. is in the 1st Species, the problem becomes more complex technically, and probably somewhat less practical musically. The present problem deals with the extremely difficult task of combining the 2nd and 3rd Species against a given C. F.

2. In terms of the ever operative "two-voice principle," the contrapuntal problem can be formulated thus:

2nd Species vs. C. F. = 2nd Species (2 notes vs. 1)
3rd Species vs. C. F. = 3rd Species (4 notes vs. 1)
3rd Species vs. 2nd Species = 2nd Species (2 notes vs. 1)
in smaller note values — quarter-notes vs. half-notes

3. While no new rules are required, it will be observed that the following restrictions (or, perhaps, more correctly 'obstacles') come more or less automatically into play:

(1) discords in the 2nd Species (i.e., in the part in half-notes) are virtually impractical in that they would set up unacceptable harmonic situations, and

(2) the Nota Cambiata and Changing-notes in the 3rd Species are likewise impractical and for the same reason.

4. The following provides a short and rather conservative example of this particular contrapuntal problem. The dotted line in the middle of each measure shows the 2nd Species relationship between the 3rd and 2nd Species.

5. A number of things can be learned from the above example:

(1) a new and more complex application of the "Discords Available" table in paragraph 3 of Chapter VI, that is in two different dimensions at once;

(2) the careful approach to all 5ths and 8ves at the first and third beats of the measure (cf. paragraphs 5, 6 and 7 of Chapter II);

(3) the proportion of 5ths to 8ves, in this case 2 to 1 — 6 5ths to 3 8ves (too many 8ves would result in an excessive number of incomplete harmonies);

(4) the melodic quality of the separate parts in spite of the limitations and obstacles (it is especially difficult to achieve a good linear design in the 2nd Species);

(5) the proportion of measures containing one harmony to those containing two harmonies. In this case, measures 2, 4 and 7 contain two harmonies while the remaining five measures (not counting the last) contain only one harmony, thereby bringing into play the traditional 3 to 5 ratio. Such proportions are, of course, subject to control by the composer.

All these considerations imply a highly controlled contrapuntal technique which can be mastered only by a great deal of practice and through a clear awareness of the structural and melodic resources available through the correct and imaginative use of discords.

6. A similar complex relationship comes about when Cpts. in the 3rd and 4th Species are written against a C. F. In this case, there are actually two 3rd Species designs in one, one of which operates in the usual way against the C. F. while the other operates against the tied notes of the 4th Species.

7. The 4th Species suspension can be used against the 3rd Species

only in one specific situation; namely, if the notes on the first and third quarters are the same, thereby being actually a variation on a whole-note:

The only possible exception to the above limitation would be if the first and third quarter-notes are definitely concords within the same harmony.

In this case the suspension actually serves as a 9 - 8 against the 'C' and as a 4 - 3 (11 - 10) against the 'A', both by implication. This effect is apt to be harmonically ambiguous and not too satisfactory musically. If used at all, it should be very seldom and worked out with great care.

8. The following illustration is a typical instance of the 3rd and 4th Species in simultaneous operation against a C. F. The dotted lines show the relation of the 3rd Species to the 4th Species.

9. Two specific situations present themselves wherein the 4 notes vs. 1 relationship between the 3rd Species and the 4th Species cannot conform to the conditions of pure 3rd Species Counterpoint:

> (1) the rule given in paragraph 8 of Chapter VI cannot always be observed (see measure 6 above); and
>
> (2) when the 3rd Species operates against a suspension, the first beat of the measure will not meet the conditions governing the third beat of a pure 3rd Species measure (see measure 2 above).

10. In minor keys, this kind of three-part writing is much more difficult due to the large number of awkward intervals within the minor scale, which set up almost impossible restrictions for the voice-leadings. Two examples follow without further comment.

EXERCISES

Select C. F. from any of the preceding chapters and write various vertical arrangements of C. F. + 2nd or 4th Species + 3rd Species.

CHAPTER XV

COUNTERPOINT IN THREE PARTS, CONCLUDED

1. The last three-part problem is that of writing three parts in the 5th Species without a given C. F.

2. The method is exactly the same as that set forth in paragraph 5 of Chapter X. The order of decisions required for each measure remains as stated therein. No additional instructions beyond those given for three-part texture in Chapters XII - XIV are necessary.

3. The following is a brief but typical example of three-part writing in the 5th Species without a given C. F. Examine each measure and reconstruct the decisions which it represents concerning choice of C. F. and contrapuntal devices.

4. Although somewhat more difficult in minor than in major, due primarily to the restricted voice-leadings when the leading-tone is involved, a contrapuntal texture of this kind is apt to become richer and darker from the expressive point of view in minor than in major. Therefore, it is important that all contrapuntal techniques be mastered in minor as well as in major.

5. Study the following example carefully, noting especially
    (1) how the raised leading-tone is introduced and left,
    (2) how the natural and raised sixth degree of the scale is treated, and
    (3) in general the voice-leadings and dissonances.

Reconstruct in detail the decisions that determine the design and content — harmonic as well as melodic — of each measure.

EXERCISES

Beginning as follows write short pieces for three voices or instruments using three-part 5th Species Counterpoint without a given C. F. Remember, this is original composition within the 5th Species resources and should represent the finest and most sincere creative effort. Allow as much length as is required to develop the contrapuntal ideas artistically, but 20 measures might be taken as minimum.

Invent original beginnings and develop them in the same way.

Chapter XVI

COUNTERPOINT IN FOUR AND MORE PARTS

1. Theoretically, counterpoint in four and more parts is no different than three-part counterpoint except that the number of constituent two-part counterpoints is increased according to the table in paragraph 3 of Chapter XII. And, the "two-voice principle" given in paragraph 4 of Chapter XII is applicable regardless of the number of parts.

2. In practice, however, it is quite another story. The difficulty of achieving correct and effective counterpoint in four and more parts increases proportionately as the number of parts is increased. Consequently, some additional freedom is necessary in the matter of
   (1) hidden 5ths and 8ves (cf. Chapter XII, paragraph 7);
   (2) unisons, and
   (3) crossing of parts.

3. When more than three voices are involved — that is to say, at least four — it can safely be assumed that hidden 5ths and 8ves are acceptable if
   (1) one of the parts progresses stepwise, and
   (2) they do not take place in the two outside voices.
Moving in the same direction to a unison is not good; and, in general, unisons should be used only if there is no practical or musically satisfactory way of avoiding them.

4. Parallel 5ths and 8ves are, of course, forbidden without exception. However, consecutive 5ths by contrary motion are occasionally encountered in multi-voiced writing (cf. Chapter II, paragraph 7). Consecutive 8ves by contrary motion, while not unknown in the music of the great composers, are rare enough to be considered inadmissible, in elementary work such as is shown in this book.

5. For multi-voiced contrapuntal writing two general rules can be formulated:
   (1) do not resolve a suspension to a note·that is doubled in some upper voice; and

(2) any vertical interval of a 4th in any constituent two-part Cpt. involving the Bass must function as a correctly treated discord.

Of these two basic rules (1) will automatically avoid the possibility of a 9 - 8 suspension between two upper voices as well as a 7 - 8 effect anywhere; while (2) avoids all incorrect six-four chords.

6. Counterpoint in four parts may be written as simply as the following example wherein three 1st Species Cpts. operate against a given C. F.[1]

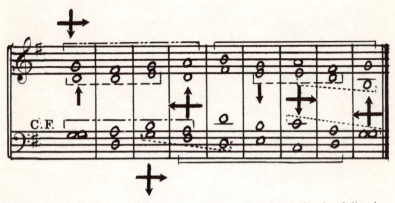

Or, it may feature Cpts. in three different Species as in the following wherein Cpts. in the 1st, 3rd, and 4th Species are written against a given C. F.

[1] For a practical application of four-part writing of this type, see CHORALE HARMONIZATION IN THE CHURCH MODES by Povl Hamburger, translated from the Danish by Hugo Norden (Boston Music Co.).

It may even achieve the ultimate in complexity by having all of the parts in the 5th Species without a given C. F., as in the following illustration.

7. Although quite possible, it is not generally practical to combine the 5th Species with continuous parts in the 2nd, 3rd, or 4th Species. The reason is that the principal feature of the 5th Species, the suspension with the ornamental resolutions, would have to be much restricted or eliminated altogether in order to avoid confusion.

8. Covered in this volume are the basic academic principles of the great art of Counterpoint. It is a highly disciplined technique, and from this point of view the rules as set forth herein constitute a norm of correct contrapuntal writing. In practical musical composition, however, composers treat this norm as their artistic requirements dictate. All academic principles are intended to help the composer, and certainly not to hinder him in his creative endeavors. When the latter seems to be the case, any knowledgeable composer will not hesitate to let his creativity take precedence over the rules. Before more advanced work is undertaken this relationship of the composer to academic theory must be put in proper perspective.

EXERCISES

I. Using any C. F. in the preceding chapters, set up and solve various problems in any of the five Species in practical combinations operating against the given C. F. The more experimentation is carried out, the more clearly it will be seen what combinations will prove successful in four and more parts.

II. Invent beginnings to be developed into compositions for voices or instruments. The following are typical.

1.

4. (5 parts — Soprano I & II, Alto, Tenor, Bass)

s.

5. (6 parts — Soprano I & II, Alto I & II, Tenor, Bass)

From the above beginnings it will be seen that the number of parts affects the nature of the harmony. As the number of parts is increased, the possibilities of writing suspensions are decreased.

Chapter XVII

TRIPLE RHYTHM

1. For purposes of contrapuntal motion, the three-beat measure is most systematically controlled when it is seen as a four-beat measure with one of the unaccented beats — that is, either the second or the fourth quarters — omitted.

Since the odd-numbered quarters are the accented ones, this will result in two kinds of three-beat measures:
  (1) those with the secondary accent on the second beat, and
  (2) those with the secondary accent on the third beat.

2. In the 1st Species this distinction is of no account since no motion is carried on within the measure, the only movement being from measure to measure.

3. But, in the 2nd Species, two different rhythms within the measure are produced in this way:

Either of these two rhythms can continue throughout an entire exercise, or they can be mixed according to the desires of the composer or according to the direction of the discords. When the second note in

109

the measure is a discord, especially if it is ascending, this would tend to be over emphasized in the first of the two rhythms shown above. Also, it might suggest to the listener that the principle given in paragraph 3 of Chapter IX was being violated, although from the purely theoretical concept shown in paragraph 1 above this would certainly not be the case.

4 To illustrate the duple-triple rhythm relationship the following conventional 2nd Species Cpt. is transformed in three ways.

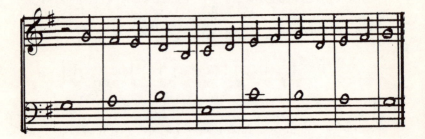

First, by means of the first rhythm shown in paragraph 3 above it will appear thus (the long ascending discords in measures 4 and 5 being of questionable value contrapuntally (cf. paragraph 3 above)),

secondly, by means of the second rhythm shown in paragraph 3, which produces smoothly flowing contrapuntal motion throughout, and

110

finally, the two rhythms in combination, the first rhythm in measures 2, 3, 6, and 7 with the second rhythm in measures 1, 4, and 5.

5. In the 3rd Species the situation is quite different. Here it can almost be said that the triple rhythm is more affected by the counterpoint than the counterpoint is by the rhythm.

6. In two specific instances only the second of the two three-beat rhythms can be considered valid; namely, when (1) an ascending passing-note or (2) an auxiliary-note appears on the second beat. Since these effects may not come on an accent (see paragraph 3 of Chapter VI), it is inevitable that the secondary accent falls on the third beat.

7. There are likewise two specific situations in which only the first of the two three-beat rhythms can be considered as being operative. These occur when the intervals 5 - 6 - 5 are written above the C. F., or 6 - 5 - 6 below the C. F. Were these two figures to be considered as operating within the second rhythm, the note on the second beat would in each case beome an upward auxiliary-note (see paragraphs 3 and 7 of Chapter VI).

8. The rule given in paragraph 12 of Chapter VI creates two specific rhythmical problems in triple rhythm. When there is a leap of a 4th or 5th from the first to the second beat the first three-beat rhythm must be considered operative, while if such a leap occurs between the second and third beats the second rhythm is being used. This will prevent a six-four chord being outlined by an accented note and its following unaccented note. It will be observed that in the second illustration shown below that no discord is possible within the 3rd Species concept of dissonance.

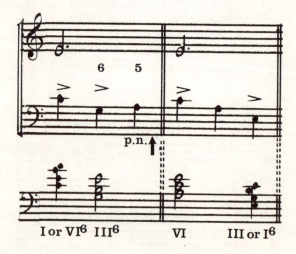

The harmonic implication possibilities are subjoined to the above illustrations (see paragraphs 17 - 22 of Chapter VI).

9. Instead of the single rhythmic figure within which a Suspension or Tie can operate in the 4th Species in duple rhythm as shown in paragraph 2 of Chapter VIII, the three-beat measure makes possible four different rhythmic possibilities on the basis of what is demonstrated in paragraph 3 above. Thus, the following convenional 7 - 6 Suspension in duple rhythm

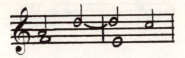

can in triple rhythm be treated in four ways thus.

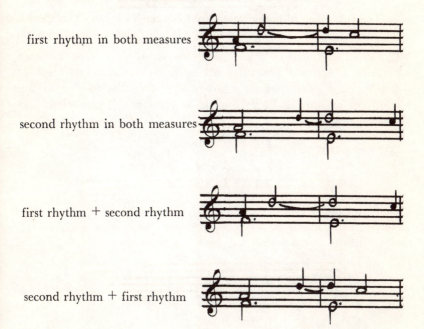

first rhythm in both measures

second rhythm in both measures

first rhythm + second rhythm

second rhythm + first rhythm

10. When suspensions are embellished with the ornamental resolutions in 5th Species treatment only the second three-beat rhythm is possible, since the ornament invariably falls on the second beat of the four-

beat measure and if this were omitted there could be no ornament to the resolution of the Suspension.

11. When eighth-notes are used apart from ornamental resolutions in the 5th Species, two figures are possible. In the following illustrations the first is in the first rhythm and the second in the second rhythm.

12. One additional rhythmic possibility exists that is at variance with the principle of omitted beats as shown in paragraph 1 above; namely, the omission of the third quarter with the result that the three-beat measure derived therefrom would consist of an accent and two unaccented beats.

This, in turn, makes possible the following figure of a quarter-note followed by two groups of eighth-notes.

EXERCISES

Using any C. F. from the preceding chapters, write Cpts. in the 2nd, 3rd, 4th, and 5th Species against same in triple rhythm.

DOUBLE COUNTERPOINT

1. "Double Counterpoint" is a Cpt. that can be played or sung either above or below the C. F., in contrast to the "Simple Counterpoint" which can be used only above or below the C. F. as is the case with all of the exercises that are demonstrated in the preceding 17 chapters. Synonyms for the term "Double Counterpoint" are "Invertible Counterpoint," "Vertical Displacement," and "Vertical Shift." [1]

2. The following brief example will show how such a Double Counterpoint structure can function.

[1] A most distinguished treatise dealing extensively with Double Counterpoint is CONVERTIBLE COUNTERPOINT IN THE STRICT STYLE by S. I. Taneiev (Bruce Humphries, Publishers).

It will be observed that in the preceding double example the C. F. remains at the same pitch while the 5th Species Cpt. is shifted downward one octave. Thus, this is Double Counterpoint at the 8ve, which henceforth will be abbreviated simply as D. C. 8. Herewith is shown how the same Cpt. can operate correctly both above and below the C. F.

3. In setting up such a structure it is necessary to work within the intervallic availabilities and limitations that are brought about by the interval of Double Counterpoint to be used. In the present case the inversions are as follows:

$$\text{D. C. 8:} \qquad \frac{1}{8} \quad \frac{2}{7} \quad \frac{3}{6} \quad \frac{4}{5} \quad \frac{5}{4} \quad \frac{6}{3} \quad \frac{7}{2} \quad \frac{8}{1}$$

By combining the two examples in paragraph 2 into one three-line system, it will appear thus:

The interval numbers above and below the C. F. correspond exactly to those in the inversion table.

4. Double Counterpoint can be invertible at any other interval besides the octave, the most commonly used being D. C. 10 and D. C. 12. The following two examples illustrate these two inversions. The student should study each measure for the contrapuntal devices contained therein.

116

D. C. 10: $\dfrac{1}{10}\ \dfrac{2}{9}\ \dfrac{3}{8}\ \dfrac{4}{7}\ \dfrac{5}{6}\ \dfrac{6}{5}\ \dfrac{7}{4}\ \dfrac{8}{3}$

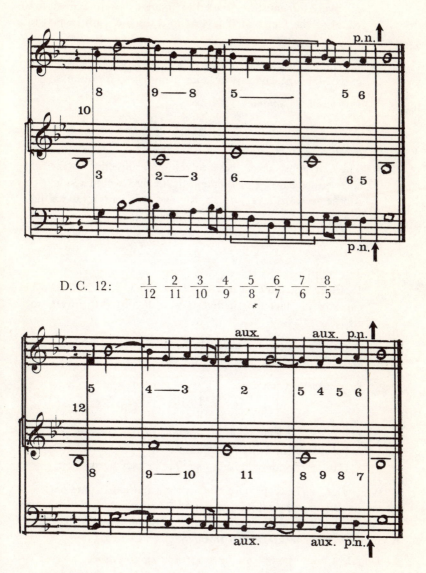

D. C. 12: $\dfrac{1}{12}\ \dfrac{2}{11}\ \dfrac{3}{10}\ \dfrac{4}{9}\ \dfrac{5}{8}\ \dfrac{6}{7}\ \dfrac{7}{6}\ \dfrac{8}{5}$

5. For these three most commonly used inversions the following brief rules can be formulated:

D. C. 8:

    1. Every 5th must be treated as though it were a discord because of the fact that it inverts to a discord (5th inverts to a 4th).

    2. An 8ve must not appear at the beginning of any measure except the first and last because it inverts to a unison.

Suspensions available:

$$\frac{4-3}{5-6} \qquad \frac{7-6}{2-3} \qquad \frac{5-4^*)}{4-5^{**})}$$

D. C. 10:

    The Cpt. must never move in the same direction as the C. F. since either parallel or hidden 5ths or 8ves would result. This is because a 3rd inverts to an 8ve, and a 6th inverts to a 5th.

Suspensions available:

$$\frac{7-6}{4-5^{**})} \qquad \frac{9-8}{2-3} \qquad \frac{6-5^{***})}{5-6}$$

D. C. 12:

    1. Every 6th must be treated as though it were a discord because of the fact that it inverts to a discord (6th inverts to a 7th).

    2. Any passage in parallel 3rds or in parallel 10ths is automatically invertible at the 12th.

Suspensions available:

$$\frac{4-3}{9-10} \text{ or } \frac{11-10}{2-3} \qquad \frac{7-6}{6-7^*)} \qquad \frac{9-8}{4-5^{**})}$$

) Provided this becomes a correctly treated discord.
    **) Provided this 5th is not diminished.
    ***) Can be considered either as a Tie or as a Suspension.

6. While D. C. 8, D. C. 10, and D. C. 12 are the most commonly employed inversions, especially in academic exercises, all inversions must be mastered if an ample contrapuntal technique is to be developed. A complete table from D. C. 8 through D. C. 15 follows:—

D. C. 8:

$$\frac{1}{8} \quad \frac{2}{7} \quad \frac{3}{6} \quad \frac{4}{5} \quad \frac{5}{4} \quad \frac{6}{3} \quad \frac{7}{2} \quad \frac{8}{1}$$

D. C. 9:

$$\frac{1}{9} \quad \frac{2}{8} \quad \frac{3}{7} \quad \frac{4}{6} \quad \frac{5}{5} \quad \frac{6}{4} \quad \frac{7}{3} \quad \frac{8}{2}$$

D. C. 10:	$\frac{1}{10}$	$\frac{2}{9}$	$\frac{3}{8}$	$\frac{4}{7}$	$\frac{5}{6}$	$\frac{6}{5}$	$\frac{7}{4}$	$\frac{8}{3}$
D. C. 11:	$\frac{1}{11}$	$\frac{2}{10}$	$\frac{3}{9}$	$\frac{4}{8}$	$\frac{5}{7}$	$\frac{6}{6}$	$\frac{7}{5}$	$\frac{8}{4}$
D. C. 12:	$\frac{1}{12}$	$\frac{2}{11}$	$\frac{3}{10}$	$\frac{4}{9}$	$\frac{5}{8}$	$\frac{6}{7}$	$\frac{7}{6}$	$\frac{8}{5}$
D. C. 13:	$\frac{1}{13}$	$\frac{2}{12}$	$\frac{3}{11}$	$\frac{4}{10}$	$\frac{5}{9}$	$\frac{6}{8}$	$\frac{7}{7}$	$\frac{8}{6}$
D. C. 14:	$\frac{1}{14}$	$\frac{2}{13}$	$\frac{3}{12}$	$\frac{4}{11}$	$\frac{5}{10}$	$\frac{6}{9}$	$\frac{7}{8}$	$\frac{8}{7}$
D. C. 15:	$\frac{1}{15}$	$\frac{2}{14}$	$\frac{3}{13}$	$\frac{4}{12}$	$\frac{5}{11}$	$\frac{6}{10}$	$\frac{7}{9}$	$\frac{8}{8}$

7. In D. C. 8, D. C. 9, D. C. 11, and D. C. 13 a special situation exists in that a concord inverts to a 4th, which can be seen at a glance from the above table. These inversions can be used freely, even in the 1st Species in two upper parts over a free bass so that by this means the 4ths become concords (see paragraph 6 of Chapter XII). The following 1st Species Cpt. in D. C. 9 and the two four-part harmonizations in which the Cpt. and C. F. serve as the two uppermost parts demonstrate in the simplest possible way how these intervallic resources may be utilized.

1st Species, D. C. 9:

119

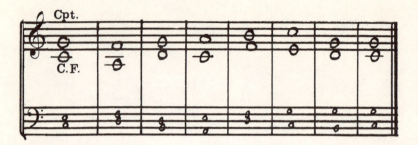

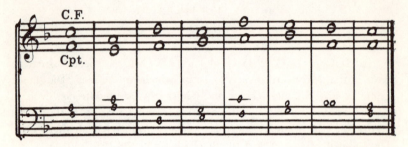

In the second of the two harmonizations shown above the C. F. and the ·Cpt. have been transposed up one octave in order to put them in a usable range for Soprano and Alto. This combination of C. F. and Cpt. could have been placed in the Alto and Tenor, thus.

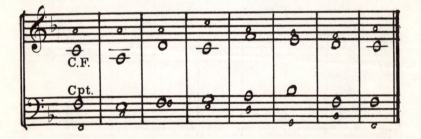

If, for any reason, such a placement of C. F. brings the harmonization out of the desired range it can, of course, be transposed to another key. In the following example the above harmonization is moved up a Major 3rd to the key of A major, wherein it is sufficiently high to permit the free bass to move more agreeably within vocal range.

8. It will be observed from the above illustrations that when free parts are added to a contrapuntal structure, the latter controls to a large extent the nature and flow of the harmonic material.

9. The sketchy observations on Double Counterpoint in the foregoing eight paragraphs must not be construed as even approaching an ample exposition of this all important branch of contrapuntal technique. They are, at best, merely a scanty introduction to acquaint the beginner with some of the most elementary problems and possibilities (see footnote to paragraph 1 above).

TRIPLE AND QUADRUPLE COUNTERPOINT

10. By "Triple Counterpoint" is meant a three-part contrapuntal structure that is so written that any of the three voices can serve as lowest, middle, or uppermost part. "Quadruple Counterpoint" is a four-part structure written in the same way. Theoretically there is no limit to the number of voices that can be combined to form a generally invertible structure, but for practical purposes four is about the limit due to the many restrictions that the inversion process imposes upon the voice-leadings.

11. Any such multi-voiced contrapuntal texture embodies a given number of two-part counterpoints in accordance with the table in paragraph 3 of Chapter XII.

12. To write Triple, Quadruple, etc. Counterpoint the following rules are necessary:
>   1. Each of the constituent two-part counterpoints must be invertible in D. C. 8 or D. C. 15.
>   2. Every 5th must be treated as though it were a discord (see paragraph 5 above, rule 1, under D. C. 8).

3. Parallel 4ths are not possible as they will invert to parallel 5ths.

4. The 9 - 8 suspension is impossible.

5. Rule 2, given under D. C. 8 in paragraph 5 above, may be relaxed to good advantage.

13. The following illustration shows a three-part structure in Triple Counterpoint in all of its six inversions. By numbering the three parts as I, II, and III it will be seen that the six inversions are

(1) I	(2) II	(3) I	(4) III	(5) II	(6) III
II	I	III	I	III	II
III	III	II	II	I	I

14. The following is a brief illustration of Quadruple Counterpoint. The student may, if he wishes, write out the other 23 inversions in the same way that the Triple Counterpoint is treated in the preceding paragraph. In this way it will be seen how the "two-part principle" stated in paragraph 4 of Chapter XII is operative in Triple and Quadruple Counterpoint.

EXERCISES

The following C. F. are of very narrow range and are especially suitable for exercises in Double Counterpoint. If desired, two or three simultaneously operating Cpts. may be written against these C. F. to bring about Triple or Quadruple Counterpoint. Of course, any C. F. from the preceding chapters may be used in the same way, but those that cover a wide range or contain leaps are apt to set up difficult problems in view of the limitations of invertible writing.